THRIFTY COOK MAIN MEALS

HOW TO COOK A MONTH'S WORTH OF HEALTHY, HEARTY MEALS ON A BUDGET

Tessa Patterson

DEDICATION

To my husband and children for all their support and for putting up with endless culinary experiments for dinner! Not to mention our dog, Matilda, for scoffing all the disasters!

Contents

THRIFTY COOK SERIES

The second book in the series was published in July 2013. *Light Meals & Lunchboxes* contains recipes for making a month's worth of lunches and light meals on a budget.
The recipes can be made for lunch, a packed lunch, or a picnic and many take only five minutes to make. Some of the recipes can be served hot, but all can be eaten cold.
The ingredients are easy to source and many of the recipes are based on leftovers.

Thrifty Cook Main Meals Two, the third book in the series was published in March 2014 and contains a month's worth of recipes for everyday cooking on a budget. Recipes include making delicious food from leftovers and cooking tasty meals from cheap, easy to source ingredients.
The list of ingredients is short and only basic cooking equipment is required to make the recipes.

The books are all available as Kindles and paperbacks from Amazon.

Website: http://www.thriftycook.co.uk

PREFACE

I have been a keen cook for many years and, towards the end of 2012, realized how much the cost of food was spiraling. I heard people in supermarkets moan about the cost of their weekly shop. I heard figures quoted on the news about inflation and calculated that some of the basic ingredients I used to feed my family had increased by nearly 50% in just under a year!

More recently in the news, we found out that almost half the food produced throughout the world is thrown away. This is mostly due to supermarkets throwing away food that has passed its "sell by date", farmers unable to harvest a particular crop due to adverse weather conditions and last, but not least, households throwing away leftover food – some of which had never even been removed from its packaging.

So many people eat readymade processed food which is not only more expensive but unhealthy too! So, I decided to share some of my tried and tested recipes. We hear almost daily in the news about the ghastly ingredients in some processed food. By making meals from scratch, not only are you going to save money but you will also know exactly what you and your family are eating.

Most of my recipes are made from seasonal fresh ingredients wherever possible, but at the time of writing it is winter in the UK and, besides root vegetables, there is not that much in season! Therefore, I have used some store cupboard ingredients to make life easier. There are also a number of main meals made with leftovers from a previous meal.

I'm a firm believer in buying good quality food and making it go further by adding extra, cheaper ingredients to "pad it out". I would far rather spend my money on quality organic produce – not only because I believe it is so much healthier and tastier, but I am very keen on animal welfare and looking after our environment without contaminating it with chemicals.

Nearly all the recipes in this book can be frozen which is especially useful when a particular crop is in season and cheap to buy. Make plenty and freeze for another day!

I hope you enjoy my creations – which won't break the bank! They are tasty, cheap and wholesome.

This book has no colour photographs which means I can keep the price down. Please look at http://www.thriftycook.co.uk for photos of each recipe.

INTRODUCTION

Before I start to list the recipes there are a few points I should like to make about planning the week's meals, buying food and useful kitchen equipment.

PLANNING

Meals for the week ahead should be easy and stress free. Work out, say at the weekend, a list of seven main meals and make up a shopping list. Try a dish or two using leftovers. For example, if you cook a roast chicken on Sunday, then use a chicken leftover dish for later in the week. Work out any days when there won't be much time to cook and choose a meal that's quick to make, or one that has been frozen.

Look in the shops and markets for offers on seasonal, local products. Look in supermarkets for "BOGOF" offers (buy one get one free), but only for the items you will need in the near future.

All the supermarkets have tempting offers, a lot of which are probably not on your list – don't buy unless you really have to or if an ingredient you use regularly is on offer. The healthier food in a supermarket tends to be nearer to the main entrance. The centre aisles are usually full of processed, sweetened, salty snacks and drinks which can be difficult to resist.

The key to cooking cheap, healthy meals is to cook from scratch. So a little planning once a week can save a lot of stress and impulse buying!

FRESH MEAT, FISH AND EGGS

I always buy meat from a local butcher, farm or farm shop – never pre-packed from a supermarket. I do this because often the meat is cheaper, you can see the cut of meat displayed and the butcher will trim, joint, score, roll, take out bones, take off skin and so on. Also, once you are a regular customer, you will find that the butcher will give advice and even discount meat, especially just before the shop closes in the evening!

I prefer to buy organic grass fed meat. In intensive farming, animals are fed routine antibiotics, growth hormones and other unpleasant ingredients in their concentrate feeds. Organic meat is more expensive but a little can go a long way and there are cheap cuts of meat, for example pork shoulder or breast of lamb which, when cooked slowly at lower temperatures, develop a wonderful flavour with no toughness. I also prefer organic meat as I believe that any animal that is reared to feed us deserves a natural life with minimum stress.

I don't cook with fish very much because it is expensive and often contaminated with mercury amongst other things. I never buy farmed fish because of the suspect list of food they are given, not to mention antibiotics again... My family and I take pure Krill Oil as a supplement, which is high in Omega 3 fatty acids and harvested from the Antarctica, the most unpolluted waters in the world. Krill is sustainable. As it is a shrimp-like creature, it is important that people with a shellfish allergy do not take this supplement. However, I have included a recipe for sardines in this book. Sardines are cheap, tasty, high in Omega 3 and low down on the food chain so they don't accumulate as many toxins as other types of larger fish.

Eggs – what a wonderful ingredient! I am fortunate enough to have a friend who has some hens and supplies me with freshly laid eggs. I would never buy battery farmed eggs – mostly because of the animal welfare aspect but also because hens should be allowed to forage outside eating grass and insects. I am convinced that their eggs and meat are healthier for us. Eggs – a meal in themselves, packed with protein, vitamins and cheap too!

VEGETABLES

I always try to buy organic vegetables if available and I grow my own too. I prefer to use vegetables in season and, if there is not much available, I'll get canned or frozen. Vegetables are so healthy and they are cheap. A small amount of meat, cheese, fish or eggs can be transformed into a stunning, tasty dish by adding a selection of vegetables. I buy most of my vegetables locally and find that they are, on the whole, much better value and fresher than from a supermarket. For example, I buy a small sack of 16.5lbs/7.5kg of potatoes from our local farm shop – the supermarkets sell potatoes in small bags which cost twice as much! So, not only do I save money but I am supporting local farmers and growers too. Main crop potatoes keep well in a cool garage or shed so a sack will last for weeks.

HERBS

I cook with herbs almost daily and I don't think I could cook without them! Leftover dishes can take on a completely new flavour by adding a handful of herbs. I grow my own herbs outside during the warmer months and more tender ones on a sunny windowsill in the winter. I do use dried herbs too over winter.

My favourite fresh herbs include rosemary (very hardy, even when left outside in the winter), basil, thyme, sage, parsley, chives, mint, oregano and tarragon. The jars of dried herbs I buy for use over winter are fennel seeds, oregano, coriander leaf (cilantro), tarragon, dill and sage.

I sow herbs in small pots in the spring. If you don't have green fingers, garden centres sell small pots of herbs and often discount them if you are buying several. If I buy herbs from a garden centre, I pot them on into bigger pots using ordinary garden soil, place them in a sunny position, water sparingly and then watch them grow!

Growing herbs at home is much more economical than buying fresh herbs in a packet. There are a number of mail order companies which I have used who supply the little plants all wrapped up individually and they arrive in perfect condition.

OILS AND FATS

My favourite cooking fats are virgin coconut oil, butter, ghee (used especially in Eastern cooking and easy to make at home – see the internet for the method), lard, beef dripping, goose fat, palm oil and cold pressed rapeseed oil (canola oil). I use olive oil but only straight from the bottle for dressings and drizzling on food that is already cooked.

I never use margarines or spreads because of the trans fatty acids contained in them. Look up how margarine is made on the internet and you too may not want to eat these fats again!

FLOUR

We don't eat much flour in our family as it is high in gluten and carbohydrates. No members of my family are gluten intolerant but I don't think that human stomachs are designed to eat large quantities of grain. I try not to serve a dish based on flour each day and sometimes use gluten free flour which seems to work well. Although I like pasta very much and especially as it is so quick to make, I haven't included any main course recipes based on pasta simply because my family hardly ever eat it! I usually make my own shortcrust pastry but always buy puff and filo pastry as they take quite a while to prepare and I have never had brilliant results making them.

SALT

I use Celtic sea salt, Himalayan rock salt or pure sea salt. I never cook with refined table salt which is processed and heated to very high temperatures. This heating alters the chemical structure. Besides anti caking agents and other chemicals, the sodium chloride percentage is higher in table salt compared to natural salt and the beneficial minerals have been depleted through processing. A little good quality natural salt, I'm sure, is positively beneficial to good health. Himalayan, Celtic and pure sea salt undergo minimal processing and contain numerous trace minerals. The other reason I use these natural salts is because the taste is far superior!

KITCHEN TOOLS AND EQUIPMENT

I used to enjoy collecting gadgets for the kitchen and many of my purchases in the past were completely unnecessary. There are several items I use regularly which save so much time. Every kitchen should have the basics. For example pots, pans, casseroles with lids, roasting pan, sharp knives, round and rectangular baking dishes, baking sheets, mixing bowls, rolling pin, colander, measuring jug, garlic crush, pastry brush, slotted spoon, balloon whisk, fish slice, wooden spoons, small hand grater, scales, salt and pepper mills etc.

Here is my list of additional favourites:-

Food processor. One that grates, slices, mixes and makes dough. It doesn't need to be expensive but make sure the bowl is nice and big.

Liquidizer. These are so useful for soups, stocks and milk shakes.

Electric hand whisk. They are brilliant for making egg whites fluffy in next to no time, whipping cream and for making lovely smooth mashed potato and other veg.

Speed peeler. Such a simple gadget but it makes peeling carrots, potatoes and other root vegetables a dream. Great for making chocolate curls too!

Salad spinner. I use mine almost daily. Any type of vegetable or salad can be washed and spun. It is important to dry salads after washing as it stops them being soggy and when using dressing, the oil sticks to the leaves when they are dry. Salad spinners are cheap and very efficient.

Large chopping board. My chopping board is very big and made from beech. I bought it from Ikea a few years ago; it cost £5 and is still as good as new.

STORE CUPBOARD

There are a range of store cupboard ingredients I always have available and, as I'm sure you will have gathered throughout this introduction, I buy organic wherever possible. My favourites include:-

Tomato purée, cans of plum tomatoes, jars of cooked whole red peppers, jars of sundried tomatoes, pulses and beans including chickpeas (garbanzo beans), black beans, red kidney beans, cannellini beans, baked beans in tomato sauce, wholegrain rice, wild rice and basmati rice, flours (as mentioned earlier), good quality mayonnaise, mango chutney, Chinese plum sauce, sweet chilli sauce, oils, green pesto sauce, bags of walnuts and almonds, peanut butter, dried herbs and spices, cans of coconut milk and packets of creamed coconut. The spices I use mostly are chilli powder, cayenne pepper, turmeric, paprika, cinnamon, nutmeg, curry powder, cumin and ground ginger.

SAUSAGE & SWEET POTATO BAKE

Hob (stovetop) and oven

Serves 4

Preparation 5 minutes/Cook for 40 minutes

Preheat oven to 200C/Fan 180/400F/Gas 6

An easy dish to make and the flavours are wonderful.

8 large sausages
1 large onion
3 garlic cloves
12oz/350g/2 cups sweet potatoes
1-2 stems of rosemary
Salt and black pepper
Oil

You will need a fairly deep oven proof roasting dish.

Peel the sweet potatoes and chop into bite sized pieces. Place them in a pan of salted water and boil gently for 5 minutes with the lid on then drain and pour into the roasting dish.

Peel and chop the onion into chunks, halve the sausages, peel and crush the garlic cloves then add all these to the sweet potatoes. Drizzle a little oil evenly over the sausages and vegetables. Take the leaves off the rosemary and chop finely. Scatter the rosemary on top. Season with salt and pepper.

Mix everything then put into the oven for about 40 minutes, shaking the dish a couple of times during cooking until the sausages and vegetables are golden and cooked through. Serve with a green vegetable.

TOMATO, GOATS' CHEESE & WALNUT TART

Vegetarian

Oven

Serves 4

Preparation 10 minutes/Cook for 15-20 minutes

Preheat oven to 200C/Fan 180/400F/Gas 6

Quick and tasty. Sundried tomatoes in jars are not expensive when only half a jar is used and they keep well. I tend to use these in the winter when fresh tomatoes are imported and tasteless! I use bought puff pastry as it is time consuming to make at home.

1 lb pack or 500g pack all butter puff pastry
4oz/100g/½ cup fresh goats' cheese
½ a small 10oz/280g jar of sundried tomatoes
2oz/50g/½ cup walnut halves
2 cloves garlic
Basil leaves – small handful
Black pepper
Olive oil for drizzling

You will need a baking sheet approx 12"x 10"/30cm x 26cm covered with a piece of baking parchment.

Roll out the pastry to fit the baking sheet and carefully place on the paper. Fold over the outer edges of the pastry to the inside, about ½"/1cm to allow the outer edges to puff up when cooking. Roughly chop the tomatoes and scatter over the pastry. Peel and crush the garlic and dot over the tomatoes. Scatter the walnuts over. Slice the cheese thinly and place evenly over the tart.

Place in the oven for about 15 minutes until risen and lightly golden. Scatter the basil leaves over as soon as the tart is cooked and drizzle with olive oil.

Slice up and serve with a green salad.

ROAST CHICKEN WITH WILD RICE

Hob (stovetop) and oven

Serves 4–6

Preparation 15 minutes/Cook for about 1 hour

Preheat oven to 200C/Fan 180/400F/Gas 6

Roast chicken is hardly a new recipe but this is not a traditional one served with roast potatoes and greens. Lemon and garlic are delicious with chicken and the rice is so easy to make and tasty too. Although a whole chicken seems expensive, an average sized chicken should provide 2 meals for 4 people. There are a number of leftover chicken recipes in this book or simply eat cold. Weight for weight, chicken is good value.

1 chicken
8oz/200g/1 cup wild rice
3 cloves garlic, unpeeled
4 spring onions (scallions)
½ a lemon
1 pint/500ml/2 cups vegetable or chicken stock
1 tsp fennel seeds (optional)
1oz/25g/⅛ cup butter or 2tbsp oil
Salt and black pepper

You will need a roasting dish and large saucepan.

Put the garlic cloves in the chicken cavity. Place the chicken in the roasting dish. Dot with butter or oil and add a little salt and pepper. Put in the oven and more or less forget about it for half an hour. Then, take it out of the oven, baste it and pop back in the oven for another half an hour.

Meanwhile, wash and slice the spring onions (scallions). When the chicken has about 10 minutes left to cook, warm through the stock or mix a stock cube with 1 pint/550ml/2 cups of boiling water. Put the rice in a saucepan and add the stock, a pinch of salt and the spring onions. Stir then simmer for about 20 minutes.

Check the chicken, the skin should be golden. Test it is cooked through by piercing behind the thigh with a sharp knife. Any juice running out should be clear and without any traces of pink. If cooked, take the chicken out of the dish, put on a plate and cover with foil to rest. Reserve the garlicky cooking juices. If it is not cooked, return to the oven for another 10-15 minutes until cooked through.

When the rice is cooked, squeeze the lemon juice over it and scatter with the fennel seeds, then place in a serving bowl. Return the pan with the chicken juices to the hob and heat right through. Pour into a jug and use to drizzle over the sliced chicken.

Any selection of vegetables will taste good with this dish.

CHICKEN, POTATO & SWEET RED PEPPER POT

Hob (Stovetop)

Serves 4

Preparation 15 minutes/Cook 20 minutes

Chicken, potatoes, red peppers and basil in one pot.

2 large or 3 small chicken breasts
1 lb/500g/3 cups new potatoes (baby potatoes)
½ a jar of roasted sweet red peppers (bell peppers or capsicum)
2 tbsp green pesto sauce
2 tbsp olive oil
Salt and black pepper
Extra basil to serve (optional)

Scrub the potatoes and put in a large pan of boiling water. Simmer for about 15 minutes or until cooked, then drain. Meanwhile, heat a griddle or frying pan (skillet), add 1 tbsp oil and cook the chicken for about 20 minutes, turning half way through until completely cooked. Roughly chop the red peppers and add to the pan with the cooked chicken.

Shake the pan with the potatoes in to break them up a little and transfer to the pan with the chicken and peppers. Add the pesto sauce and 1 tbsp olive oil. Season with salt and pepper. Stir everything so that the chicken and potatoes are coated in oil and pesto. Put in a serving dish and scatter with a few basil leaves.

Good with a crunchy green salad or peas.

OVEN BAKED TORTILLA

Vegetarian

Oven and hob (stovetop)

Serves 4-6

Preparation 10 minutes/Cook 35 minutes

Preheat oven to 180C/Fan 160/350F/Gas 4

This dish is fantastic served warm or cold. Add additional leftover vegetables if you have any to make it go further

4oz/100g/1 cup Cheddar cheese
4 eggs
2 fresh sweet peppers (any colour) or use cooked ones from a jar (bell peppers or capsicum)
4 spring onions (scallions)
8oz/200g/1 cup boiled potatoes
1 large garlic clove
8fl oz/200ml/1 cup soured cream
Oil or butter for frying
Salt and black pepper

Grease an 8" x 12"/20cm x 30cm oven proof dish. Grate the cheese and leave to one side. Peel and crush the garlic, wash and slice the spring onions (scallions) and wash and chop the peppers into bite sized chunks, discarding the seeds.

Heat a tablespoon or so of oil or butter in a frying pan (skillet). Add the garlic, spring onion and peppers. Stir over gentle heat for about 5 minutes, or until slightly softened.

In a bowl, add the eggs, soured cream, seasoning and half the cheese. Mix well. Place the cooked potatoes over the base of an oven proof dish. Put all the other ingredients in, except the cheese, and spread around evenly. Add any other leftover vegetables you may have then scatter over the remaining cheese.
Put in the oven for about 25-30 minutes until slightly risen and golden. Allow to cool a little before serving. Serve warm or cold with a salad.

A BIT OF EVERYTHING PIE

Oven

Serves 4

Preparation 10 minutes/Cook 25-30 minutes

Preheat oven to 180C/Fan 160/350F/Gas 4

This pie is simply made from leftovers. It can be made from any roast leftover meat together with all the vegetables served originally and gravy. It is an easy meal to make and satisfying too. After making "Bubble and Squeak" dozens of times, I thought there must be some other tasty way of using up a leftover roast meal!

A couple of handfuls of leftover cooked meat
1 ½ lbs/700g/3 cups of leftover vegetables e.g. potatoes, carrots, parsnips, peas, broccoli (calabrese)
1 can of baked beans (cannellini or any other cooked beans) if there aren't enough vegetables
¼ pint/150ml/½ cup of left over gravy – instant's fine also
8oz/200g shortcrust pastry (see below) or buy ready made
1 beaten egg or a little milk to glaze

You will need a fairly deep oven proof ceramic dish (any shape) about 12"x9"/30x23 cm. Grease the dish with a little oil or butter to stop the pie from sticking to the sides.

Chop the meat into bite sized pieces and spread over the base of the dish. Chop the vegetables into chunks and scatter over. Add a can of baked beans if there doesn't look like there is enough. Drizzle gravy over. Press the pie contents down lightly to make the top even.

Roll out the pastry to roughly fit the dish. Don't worry about being precise. Place the pastry over the meat and vegetable mixture. If the pastry is too big then scrunch up the edges a little to make it fit the dish. Make a couple of slits in the pastry with a sharp knife to allow the steam to escape while cooking.

Brush the pie with a little beaten egg or milk and bake in the oven for about 30-40 minutes until the pastry is lightly golden.

Shortcrust pastry

**4 oz/100g/½ cup butter, 8oz/200g/2 cups plain flour, A pinch of salt
2 tbsp cold water**

Sieve the flour into a bowl. Chop the butter into pieces and add to the bowl. Add the salt. With clean hands, gently rub the butter into the flour with your finger tips until the mixture looks like breadcrumbs (or put the ingredients into a food processor and pulse until everything is mixed). If you have used a food processor, put the mixture into a mixing bowl. Add the water and mix with a round bladed knife until the mixture forms a dough. Leave to one side until ready to roll out.

BEEF, SWEET PEPPER & POTATO BAKE

Hob (stovetop) and oven
Serves 4
Preparation 15 minutes/Cook 20-30 minutes
Preheat oven to 180C/Fan 160/350F/Gas 4

I have used 2 roasted red peppers from a jar for this dish but if fresh sweet peppers are in season and reasonably priced, by all means use these instead. This is a layered dish of beef, potatoes, red peppers and cheese, baked in the oven.

1lb/500g/2 cups minced beef (ground beef)
2lbs/1kg/6 cups (approx) potatoes
2 garlic cloves
2 roasted sweet red peppers from a jar or fresh (bell peppers or capsicum)
4oz/100g/1 cup cheddar or other melting cheese
3 eggs beaten
2 heaped tbsp natural yogurt
Salt and pepper
Butter or oil for frying and greasing– about 2tbsp

Peel the potatoes and cut into ¼"/1cm slices. Simmer them in a pan of boiling water for about 15 minutes or until slightly soft. Drain. Meanwhile, butter an ovenproof baking dish approx 10"x 12"/25 x 30cm. Peel and crush the garlic cloves. Melt the butter or oil in a large frying pan (skillet) then add the beef and garlic. If using fresh peppers, chop into chunks, discard the seeds and add to the pan. Cook for about 8 minutes stirring occasionally to break up the meat.

Place half of the potatoes in the dish, spreading out to cover the base. Place the red peppers over the potatoes. Spread the beef and garlic over the peppers. Finish with a final layer of potatoes.

Mix the eggs and yogurt in a bowl and spread over the potatoes. Season. Grate the cheese all over the top and place in the oven for about 20-30 minutes until the cheese is golden and bubbling.

Serve with salad or any green vegetable.

BUTTERNUT SQUASH CURRY

Vegetarian

Hob (Stovetop)

Serves 4-6

Preparation 10 minutes/Cook 20 minutes

Squash, chickpeas (garbanzo beans), a little spice and something to make the flavours richer and thicken the curry – peanut butter! A one pot meal.

1 butternut squash
1 large onion
14oz/400g can of chickpeas (garbanzo beans) drained
2 large tbsp of peanut butter
2-3 tsp chilli powder, flakes or a fresh chilli finely sliced
1 tsp cumin
2-3 tbsp oil (preferably coconut oil as this adds to the flavour)
Coriander (cilantro) to garnish if available

Put the oil in a large pan or casserole. Peel and chop the onion and add to the pan. Cook on medium heat for about 5 minutes to soften, stirring occasionally.

Peel and chop the squash into bite sized pieces. Add the chilli, cumin, chickpeas and squash to the pan. Stir to combine. Add enough boiling water to almost cover the vegetables and spices. Stir in the peanut butter.

Put a lid on, slightly askew and leave to simmer, stirring every now and then for about 15-20 minutes or until the squash is tender.

Put into a serving dish and scatter with coriander (cilantro) if using.

Serve with either basmati rice, flatbreads, puppodums or a mixture. Also tastes good with a cucumber salad or sliced bananas.

SAUSAGE & APPLE PLAIT

Oven and hob (Stovetop)

Serves 4

Preparation 15-20 minutes/Cook for 30 minutes

Preheat oven to 200C/Fan 180/400F/Gas 6

Sausage, apple, onion and mustard in pastry. I always use sausages rather than pre-packed sausage meat as they are a little cheaper and have more texture.

8oz/200g shortcrust pastry either bought or homemade
8 thick sausages or 1 lb/500g pack sausage meat
1 large onion
2 dessert apples
1 heaped tsp of mustard (whichever type you prefer)
1 oz/25g/⅛ cup butter
1 egg beaten
1 tsp dried herbs e.g. sage or thyme (optional)

Peel and finely chop the onion. Melt the butter in a pan, add the onion and cook on gentle heat until soft, stirring occasionally. Put the onion into a mixing bowl. Add the egg, mustard and herbs (if using). Peel and chop the apples and add to the onion mixture. Stir.

With a sharp knife, make a slit down the length of each sausage and squeeze the meat away from the skin. Add the sausage meat to the bowl and mix everything well.

Roll out the pastry into a rectangle about ¼"/5mm thick. Set the pastry in front of you as if it were in landscape rather than portrait. Imagine it divided vertically into three sections and line the sausage mixture so that it fills the middle section of the pastry, leaving a gap of about ½"/1.3cm at the top and bottom.

Slice the pastry on either side with a sharp knife in a herringbone pattern so that the strips are about 1"/2.5cm wide. With a pastry brush, dampen the pastry using a little water. Starting at the top, fold each strip of pastry over the sausage mixture, alternating sides, to form a "plait". If you like the pastry golden, brush the completed sausage plait with a little milk or beaten egg.

Bake in the centre of the oven until piping hot and golden.

MEATLOAF WITH HORSERADISH

Oven

Serves 4-6

Preparation 10 minutes/Cook 90 minutes

Preheat oven to 180C/Fan 160/350F/Gas 4

Quick and easy to prepare. The horseradish and herbs really add to the flavour

2 lbs/1kg/4 cups minced beef (ground beef)
1 egg
1 onion
1 large clove garlic
2oz /50g/1 cup breadcrumbs
1 tbsp horseradish sauce
1 tbsp thyme leaves
Salt and black pepper

Grease a 2lb/1kg loaf tin. Peel and finely chop the onion, crush the garlic clove and put in a large mixing bowl. Add all the other ingredients and stir well with a large spoon until everything is mixed. Pack the mixture into the loaf tin and cover with a piece of foil or baking parchment. Place in the oven for about an hour then take off the foil. Put back in the oven for another 30 minutes.

When cooked, take out of the oven and leave for about 10 minutes to set before serving. This will help to stop it breaking up when sliced.

Serve with potatoes, carrots and a green vegetable.

SLOW ROASTED SHOULDER OF PORK

Oven and hob (Stovetop)

Serves 4-6 with leftovers

Preparation 10 minutes/Cook about 6 hours

Preheat oven to 220C/Fan 200/425F/Gas 7 for 30 minutes

Then reduce heat to 140C/Fan 120/275F/Gas 1 for 5 hours

Increase heat to 190C/Fan 170/375F/Gas 5 for last half hour

A tasty and cheap cut of meat which needs long, slow cooking. Ask your butcher to score the skin to make crackling. I cook this joint with the bone in as I think it gives more flavour. Make at the weekend and share with family or friends.

4 lbs/roughly 2 kg shoulder of pork
3 large or 6 small onions
2 tbsp oil
2 sprigs rosemary, discard stems and finely chop leaves
Salt and pepper
2 tbsp flour
½ pint/250ml/1 cup stock – pork, chicken or vegetable

Peel and chop the onions in half and place in the bottom of a roasting tin. Place the pork, skin side up, on top of the onions. Rub the skin with oil and grind salt over it. Put in a hot oven for 30 minutes to heat the meat through. Lower the oven temperature, cover the pork loosely with foil and cook for about 5 hours.

After 5 hours, remove the pork from the oven. Turn the oven up. Take off the foil and put the pork on a plate or board. Scatter the rosemary over the onion. Place the pork back on top of the onions and put back in the oven for about 30 minutes or until the crackling (skin) is crispy. If you want to serve roast vegetables, cook them in a separate roasting tin.

When the pork is cooked, transfer to a plate to rest for about 20 minutes covered with the foil. Put the onions in a dish and keep warm.

To make gravy, put the roasting tin on the hob and stir the meat juices. Add the flour and gradually add the stock stirring constantly until the gravy thickens. The gravy will be flavoured with the onions and rosemary.

To serve the meat, take the crackling off and chop or cut into chunks. Use a fork to take the meat off the bone.

SPINACH & MUSHROOM PANCAKES

Vegetarian

Oven and hob (Stovetop)

Serves 4

Preparation 15 minutes/Cook for 15-20 minutes

Preheat oven to 200C/Fan 180/400F/Gas 6

Tasty, savoury pancakes. I use frozen spinach but use fresh by all means.

Batter

4 oz/100g plain/1 cup flour, 1 egg, ½ pint/300ml/1 cup milk
Pinch of salt, Oil for frying

Pancake Filling

1 lb/500g/2 ½ cups frozen leaf spinach, thawed
4 large flat mushrooms
4 oz/100g/1 cup cheddar, parmesan or other cheese, grated
Salt and pepper
1 oz/25g/⅛ cup butter
4 tbsp cream

Grease an ovenproof dish – approximately 13" x 9"/33 x 23cm.

Wipe the mushrooms with a cloth or paper towel then slice them fairly thinly. Melt the butter in a large saucepan and add the mushrooms, stirring until the liquid has evaporated. Add the spinach, stirring until it is heated through. Take the pan off the heat. Add half the grated cheese and stir into the mixture.

Make the batter: Sieve the flour into a mixing bowl. Add the salt. Crack in the egg and mix everything, preferably with a balloon whisk. Add the milk then beat the batter until smooth.

Put a small amount of oil into a frying pan (skillet) and allow the pan to become hot. Pour a quarter of the batter into the frying pan. When the bottom of the pancake becomes golden, flip over and cook the other side. Place the cooked pancake on a plate.

Put quarter of the spinach and mushroom mixture along the centre of the pancake. Roll up the pancake and put in the ovenproof dish. Repeat with the other 3 pancakes. Put the rest of the grated cheese evenly over the top of each pancake and drizzle with cream. Place in the oven for about 15 minutes until the cheese is bubbling.

Serve with crusty bread and tomato salad.

SAUSAGE & RICE HOTPOT

Hob (Stovetop) and grill (broiler)

Serves 4

Preparation 15 minutes/Cook 30 minutes

A one pot meal made with sausages, onion, garlic, rice and herbs.

8 thick sausages
10 oz/300g/1½ cups long grain or wild rice
2 large garlic cloves
1 oz/25g/⅛ cup butter
1 pint/600ml/2 cups stock
2 heaped tsp mustard
1 tbsp of thyme or parsley
Salt and pepper

Place the sausages under a hot grill (broiler), or in a large frying pan (skillet). Turn them occasionally so they brown on each side. This will take about 15 minutes. Meanwhile, peel and slice the onion and crush the garlic cloves.

Put the butter in a casserole and melt. Add the onion. Stir every now and then for about 10 minutes until softened. Add the garlic. Put the mustard and herbs into the casserole. Stir. Put the browned sausages into the casserole and add the rice and stock. Season with salt and plenty of black pepper and stir well. Simmer for about 30 minutes until the rice is soft, stirring occasionally so that the mixture doesn't stick to the base.

Serve with a green vegetable such as peas, broccoli (calabrese), green beans or cabbage.

CRISPY CHICKEN DRUMSTICKS

Oven

Serves 4

Preparation 5 minutes/Cook for 45 minutes

Preheat oven to 180C/Fan 160/350F/Gas 4

Spicy, crispy chicken drumsticks cooked in the oven. Very easy to make and always a winner.

8 chicken drumsticks
4 tbsp plain flour
2-3 tsp paprika
Salt (1 tsp) and black pepper
3 tbsp oil

Put the oil in a roasting tin. Place the flour, paprika, salt and pepper in a polythene freezer bag. Put 4 drumsticks into the bag, twist the top of the bag and shake well. Shake excess flour off the drumsticks and put them in the roasting dish. Repeat with the remaining 4 drumsticks.

Put the tin in the oven for about 45 minutes, turning the chicken over half way through cooking until crispy and golden.

Serve with sautéed potatoes, sweetcorn, coleslaw or salad.

HOMEMADE PIZZA

Vegetarian

Oven and Hob (Stovetop)

Serves 4 (makes 2 large or 4 smaller pizzas)

Preparation 15 minutes (plus 30 minutes for rising) /Cook 15 minutes

Preheat oven to 220C/Fan 200/425F/Gas 7

One of my family's favourites! Easy to make, especially after a little practice and even easier if you have a food processor! Great for meat eaters or vegetarians depending on the toppings used. My family like mozzarella with cooked and sliced mushrooms on top. When the pizzas are cooked, I scatter large basil leaves on top and drizzle garlic oil all over. Delicious!

20 oz/550g/5 cups strong white bread flour
4 tsp dried yeast
2 tsp salt
12 fl oz/350ml/1½ cups warm water
3 tbsp oil
1 can of plum tomatoes
1 tbsp tomato purée
1 clove garlic
Mozzarella cheese – grated or sliced
1 tsp oregano
Additional toppings e.g. mushrooms, pepperoni, large basil leaves, chicken, garlic oil

First of all, make the dough: Put the flour, salt, yeast and 2 tbsp oil in a mixing bowl or the bowl of a food processor. Mix. Slowly add the warm water and mix in thoroughly. If using a processor, put on full speed until the dough forms a ball and process for about 5 minutes. If mixing by hand, put the dough onto a floured board and knead for about 10 minutes, pushing, stretching and turning it until the dough becomes soft and pliable. Lightly oil a clean mixing bowl. Place the dough in the bowl, cover with a tea cloth and leave for about 30 minutes in a warm place to rise.

To make the tomato sauce, put 1tbsp oil in a saucepan. Crush the garlic clove into the pan and stir for about 30 seconds. Add the whole can of plum tomatoes and the tomato purée. Break up the plum tomatoes with a wooden spoon or a potato masher. Simmer on the hob for about 10 minutes, stirring occasionally.

Once the dough has risen to about double in size, divide into 2 or 4 pieces (depending on whether you want 2 large pizzas or 4 smaller ones). On a lightly floured board, roll out the dough to form a circle (or a rectangle). Gently, stretch the dough with your hands then continue rolling until the dough is quite thin. Place on a baking sheet. Repeat with the remaining pieces of dough. Spread the tomato sauce over each pizza. Cover each one with mozzarella. Place your chosen toppings on top (or leave as a "Margherita" pizza) and sprinkle with oregano. Put the pizzas in the oven for about 10 minutes, swapping them from top to bottom shelf half way through cooking to make sure that both the base and the top are cooked.

If you want to freeze the pizzas, only cook them for about 5 minutes, cool completely and then freeze.

OLIVE, YELLOW PEPPER & CHEESE FLAN

Vegetarian

Oven and hob (Stovetop)

Serves 4-6

Preparation 20 minutes/Cook for 30 minutes

Preheat oven to 200C/Fan 180/400F/Gas 6

This flan is delicious served warm rather than piping hot. Use really good plump black olives for the best flavour. You can use pitted olives, but whole olives taste so much better! A tasty flan to eat cold for lunch the next day. You can use a readymade pastry case if you prefer.

Pastry

6 oz/175g/1½ cups plain flour
3 oz/85g/½ cup butter

Filling

2 yellow peppers
2 spring onions (scallions)
2 eggs
4 fl oz/100ml/½ cup cream
2 fl oz/50ml/¼ cup milk
4 oz/100g/1 cup olives
3 oz/85g/¾ cup grated cheese
1 tbsp oil
Black pepper

Make the pastry. Sift the flour into a bowl, chop the butter into pieces and add to the flour. Rub together with your fingertips until the mixture looks like breadcrumbs. Add 2-3 tbsp cold water and cut and stir with a round bladed knife until the pastry forms a stiff dough. Leave to rest and prepare the filling.

Wash and chop the yellow pepper into chunks. Put the oil in a pan, add the peppers and cook over gentle heat for about 5 minutes until slightly softened. Put the eggs, milk and cream in a bowl and beat until combined. Add the peppers, olives, cheese, spring onions (scallions) and some black pepper. Stir.

Roll the pastry out on a lightly floured surface and place in a greased, deep 8"/20cm flan tin. Prick the base of the flan with a fork. Lay a sheet of baking parchment over the pastry case and cover with a sheet of foil. Press the foil onto the base and sides of the flan case to stop it losing its shape during cooking. Put the flan in the oven for about 15 minutes.

Take the flan out of the oven and allow to cool slightly. Carefully peel off the foil and paper. Pour the filling into the flan case and cook in the oven for about 30 minutes until the filling is slightly set. Leave to cool a little before serving.

Serve with new (baby) potatoes and a salad.

ROAST BELLY PORK

Oven

Serves 4-6 with leftovers

Preparation 5 minutes/Cook about 2 hours

Preheat oven to 220C/Fan 200/425F/Gas 7 for 30 minutes

Then reduce heat to 180C/Fan 160/350F/Gas 4 for about 1 ½ hours

A really tasty, economical roast.

1 thick end pork belly
Sea salt and black pepper

Rub the skin with sea salt and black pepper. Place in a roasting pan, skin side up and cook in the oven for 30 minutes. Turn the oven temperature down and continue roasting for 1 ½ hours or until the crackling (skin) is very crispy and golden. If the crackling isn't crispy, turn the oven temperature up again and cook for a little longer.

Take out of the oven and leave for about 15 minutes to rest. Take the crackling off and cut into chunks. Carve the meat into thick slices to serve.

Good with mashed potatoes, green vegetables and apple sauce.

CHICKEN WITH SWEETCORN

Hob (Stovetop)

Serves 4

Preparation 10 minutes/Cook 15 minutes

A tasty dish using leftover cooked chicken. If there are any leftovers with this dish, refrigerate until needed then put in a pan with a little milk or cream on low heat, stirring until piping hot and use as a pasta sauce.

12 oz/350g/3 cups leftover cooked chicken
2 celery sticks
3 spring onions (scallions)
12 oz/350g/1½ cups frozen or canned sweetcorn
2 oz/50g/¼ cup butter
½ pint/250ml/1 cup milk
4 tbsp plain flour
Salt and pepper

Wash and slice the celery and spring onions (scallions). Melt the butter in a large saucepan and add the chicken. Stir for a minute or two. Add the sweetcorn, spring onions and celery. Stir until warmed through. Season. Add the flour then gradually add the milk, stirring all the time. Cook on gentle heat, stirring until the mixture is hot and bubbling, for about 10 minutes. If it looks dry, add a little more milk.

Serve on baked potatoes or with new (baby) potatoes and green vegetables.

SAUSAGE & CABBAGE CASSEROLE

Oven and hob (Stovetop)

Serves 4

Preparation 20 minutes/Cook 45 minutes

Preheat oven to 180C/Fan 160/350F/Gas 4

A one pot comfort meal.

8 sausages
1 large onion
1 spring cabbage (or any dark green cabbage)
1 cooking apple
1 oz/25g/⅛ cup butter
1-2 tsp wholegrain mustard (or any mustard you have)
Rosemary sprigs
Salt and pepper

Peel and chop the onion. Wash, dry and slice the cabbage discarding the tough stem. Take the leaves off the rosemary stems and roughly chop. Put a casserole on medium heat. Add the sausages and stir every now and then until they are just browned. Remove the sausages to a plate, put the butter in the casserole and add the onion and rosemary. Stir every now and then for about 5 minutes until softened.

Peel, core and slice the apple. Put the cabbage, apple and mustard in the casserole. Season and then pile the sausages on top. Add a couple of tablespoons of water. Put a lid on the casserole and pop in the oven for about 30 minutes. Great with mashed potato.

STICKY CHICKEN THIGHS IN PLUM SAUCE

Oven

Serves 4

Preparation 5 minutes/Cook for 1 – 1 ½ hours

Preheat oven to 200C/Fan 180/400F/Gas 6

Crispy chicken in a sweet plum sauce.

8 chicken thighs
4 tbsp Chinese plum sauce (bought or homemade)
Herbs – coriander (cilantro), basil or oregano to serve (optional)
2 tbsp oil or a small knob of butter
Salt and black pepper

Trim the thighs of excess fat and place skin side down in a roasting tin. Drizzle with the oil, or dot with butter. Sprinkle a little salt and black pepper over each thigh and place in oven.

After about 30 minutes, turn the thighs over. Depending on the chicken, you may need to drain off excess water at this stage. Allow to roast for another 30 minutes then take out of the oven. Spoon ½ tablespoon of plum sauce over each thigh then return to the oven until cooked through (about an extra 10-20 minutes depending on the size of the thighs).

When cooked, place on a serving dish and scatter herbs over if you like. Serve with rice or potatoes and some green vegetables or salad.

COURGETTE, TOMATO & CHEESE BAKE

Vegetarian

Oven and hob (stove top)

Serves 4

Preparation 10 minutes/Cook for 20-30 minutes

Preheat oven to 180C/Fan 160/350F/Gas 4

Flavours of the Mediterranean. Baked vegetables with a gooey cheese sauce on top.

1 lb/500g/3 cups courgettes (zucchini)
1 onion
3 cloves garlic
1 can plum tomatoes
1 tsp tomato purée
2 eggs
6 oz/175g/¾ cup full fat plain yoghurt
4 oz/100g/1 cup grated cheese
Salt and black pepper
A little oil or butter for frying
Basil leaves to garnish (optional)

Peel and slice the onion finely. Crush the garlic. Wash the courgettes (zucchini) and chop into small chunks. Melt the butter or oil in a casserole and add the onions. Cook on low heat for about 10 minutes, stirring occasionally, until softened. Add the garlic and mix well. Add the courgettes, can of tomatoes and tomato purée. Season. Simmer for about 10-15 minutes stirring every now and then.

Meanwhile, mix the yoghurt and eggs together in a bowl. When the vegetables have been simmering for 10 minutes, check that the courgettes are almost soft. If not, cook for another 5 minutes. Take the casserole off the heat and dollop the yoghurt mixture over the vegetables then cover with grated cheese. Bake in the oven for about 15 minutes or until the cheese is golden and bubbling.

Serve with crusty bread.

SARDINES WITH PARSLEY & LEMON

Grill (broiler) or frying pan (skillet)

Serves 4

Preparation 5 minutes/Cook 6 minutes

Very quick, healthy and thrifty! Make sure that any additional vegetables are almost ready before cooking the sardines as they cook in minutes. Ask your fishmonger to gut, scale and bone the fish.

8 large or 12 small fresh sardines, gutted, scaled and boned (or see below)
A bunch of parsley
1 lemon
1 tbsp oil – if using a frying pan

Wash and chop the parsley. Zest the lemon skin then chop the lemon in half. Preheat the grill (broiler) to its hottest setting. Rinse the sardines and pat dry. If using a frying pan (skillet), heat the oil and when hot, add the sardines. If using the grill, lay the sardines in the grill pan. Sprinkle half the parsley, the lemon zest and squeeze half the lemon juice over the sardines. Cook for 2-3 minutes then turn the fish over, scatter over the remaining parsley, zest and lemon juice.

To check if the sardines are cooked through, the skin should be a golden colour and if you pinch the skin around the middle part of the fish, it should pull away easily.

Serve immediately with vegetables or salad and crusty bread.

Note: To fillet the sardines yourself: Take the raw fish and hold belly side down. Press on the spine until you feel the bones separate from the flesh. Do not use a knife but push your thumb between the bones and flesh and run it along the length of the fish. The spine and rib cage should come out easily. But practice makes perfect!

HAM ENDS WITH TOMATOES & BEANS

Hob (stove top)

Serves 4

Preparation 15 minutes/Cook 30 minutes

A very filling, cheap meal and packed with flavour. Some butchers will even give away bacon ends (ham ends) for free! In the UK, these are also known as bacon misshapes or bacon bits.

2 lbs/900g/4 cups bacon ends (ham ends or bacon lardons)
1 large onion
3 cloves garlic
1 can plum tomatoes
1 can cannellini beans or chickpeas (garbanzo beans)
½ pint/275ml/1 cup of stock or water
A large handful of small pasta shapes (or 1 lb/450g/2½ cups new (baby) potatoes scrubbed)
2 tsp tomato purée
A little oil, about 1 tbsp, or butter for frying
Black pepper

Peel and slice the onion. Crush the garlic. Put the butter or oil in a casserole or large heavy saucepan and melt. Put the onions in and cook on gentle heat for about 10 minutes, stirring every now and then. Add the garlic and mix.

Trim the really fatty bits off the bacon (ham) and add the bacon to the casserole. Add the drained beans, the whole can of tomatoes, tomato purée, stock or water and black pepper. If using potatoes, rather than pasta, add the potatoes too.

Simmer for about 15 minutes, stirring occasionally then add the pasta. Stir well and continue to simmer for another 15 minutes, stirring a little, until the pasta is cooked through.

I like this simply served with a crunchy green salad but a little grated cheese on top of the finished meal is delicious!

CHUNKY VEGETABLE CASSEROLE

Vegetarian

Hob (stove top)

Serves 4

Preparation 15 minutes/Cook 30 minutes

Filling, healthy and economical.

1 ¾ pints/1 litre/4 cups hot chicken or vegetable stock (vegetarian version)
1 large onion
2 cloves garlic
2 sticks celery
¼ cabbage
2 large carrots
1 rounded tsp tomato purée
1 oz/25g/⅛ cup butter
4 oz/100g/1 cup small pasta shapes
4 oz/100g/1 cup grated cheese
Black pepper

Peel and slice the onion finely. Crush the garlic. Wash the celery and slice. Wash and slice the cabbage thinly. Scrub the carrots, top and tail them and chop into dice.

In a large casserole or heavy saucepan, melt the butter. Add the onions and cook gently for about 5 minutes stirring every now and then. Add the garlic and mix in. Add all the vegetables, pasta, tomato purée and a few twists of black pepper.

Simmer for about 20-30 minutes until the vegetables are soft. If the dish looks too thick, add a little water or stock.

Serve in bowls and sprinkle with grated cheese. A slice of bread is all you'll need with this casserole.

CHILLI BEEF WITH CHOCOLATE

Hob (stove top)

Serves 4

Preparation 5 minutes/Cook 30 minutes

An unusual and different combination of flavours. This dish is ideal for people who like beef and chillies but don't like or can't eat kidney beans.

1 lb/450g/½ cup minced beef (ground beef)
1 red onion (or white if you don't have any red onions)
3 cloves garlic
1-2 tsp chilli powder/flakes or a fresh red chilli
1 oz/25g/¼ cup dark chocolate
1 can plum tomatoes
Oil or butter – about 1 tbsp
Salt and black pepper

Peel and finely chop the onion. Crush the garlic cloves. Chop the chocolate into chunks. If using a fresh chilli, wash and slice very finely.

Melt the oil or butter in a casserole or heavy pan on medium heat. Add the onion. Stir for a couple of minutes then add the garlic. Stir for another minute or two.

Add the minced beef, chilli, chocolate and tomatoes. Season with salt and pepper.

Cook on medium heat, uncovered for about 30 minutes, stirring every now and then.

Serve on a baked potato or with rice and a simple green salad.

RED ONION & GOATS' CHEESE TART

Vegetarian

Oven

Serves 4-6

Preparation 10 minutes/Cook for 15 minutes

Preheat oven to 200C/Fan 180/400F/Gas 6

A yummy combination of flavours on puff pastry.

1 lb/500g pack of all butter puff pastry
4 large red onions
4 oz/100g/ ½ cup goats' cheese
2 oz/50g/¼ cup butter
2 tbsp olive oil
Thyme sprigs or oregano
Black pepper

Peel and slice the onions. Melt the butter in a large saucepan. Add the onions and cook on medium heat stirring occasionally for about 10 minutes or until the onions are soft. Do not let them brown or stick to the base of the pan.

Take a large baking sheet and either grease it with a little butter or oil, or cut out a piece of baking parchment to fit the baking sheet.

Roll out the pastry to fit the baking sheet and carefully place on top. Spread the onions evenly over the pastry allowing a margin of about 1"/2.5cm around the edges of the pastry. Crumble or slice the goats' cheese over the onions. Scatter the thyme or oregano leaves over the top.

Turn the edges of the pastry in, towards the centre of the tart and bake in the oven for about 15 minutes until the pastry is golden. When cooked, drizzle with olive oil.

I serve this with a mixed green salad and sliced tomatoes.

CHICKEN & TARRAGON PANCAKES

Oven and hob (stove top)

Serves 4

Preparation 10 minutes/Cook for 15-20 minutes

Preheat oven to 200C/Fan 180/400F/Gas 6

Savoury chicken and tarragon pancakes in a creamy sauce. If you like, you can add some lightly cooked mushrooms to make the pancakes more substantial.

Batter

4 oz/100g/1 cup plain flour
1 egg
½ pint/300ml/1 cup milk
Pinch of salt
Oil for frying

Pancake Filling

3-4 chicken breasts or 6-8 thighs (depending on size)
2 garlic cloves
4 tbsp milk
4 tbsp cream
1-2 tsp fresh or dried tarragon
1 tbsp flour
1 oz/25g/⅛ cup butter
Salt and black pepper

Grease an ovenproof dish – approximately 13" x 9"/33 x 23cm.

Chop the chicken flesh into strips. Crush the garlic cloves. Melt the butter in a large frying pan (skillet). Add the chicken and cook on medium heat, stirring, for about 4 minutes. Add the garlic and stir for another minute. Add the flour, tarragon and milk. Season with salt and black pepper. Stir until the sauce thickens slightly then take off the heat.

Make the batter: Sieve the flour into a mixing bowl. Add the salt. Crack in the egg and mix everything, preferably with a balloon whisk. Add the milk then beat the batter until smooth.

Put a small amount of oil into a frying pan (skillet) and allow the pan to become hot. Pour a quarter of the batter into the frying pan. When the bottom of the pancake becomes golden, flip over and cook the other side.

Place the cooked pancake on a plate. Put quarter of the chicken mixture along the centre of the pancake. Roll up the pancake and put in the ovenproof dish. Repeat with the other 3 pancakes. Pour a tablespoon of cream evenly over each pancake.

Cook in the oven for about 15 minutes until golden.

Serve with vegetables or salad.

CHEESE & HAM PUFFS

Hob (stovetop)

Serves 4

Preparation 10 minutes/Cook 15 minutes

A simple dish to make using a frying pan (skillet) and mixing bowl.

2 lbs/1 kg or about 4 medium sized floury potatoes such as Maris Piper
4 oz/100g/1 cup Cheddar or good melting cheese
1 small onion
4oz/100g/½ cup cooked ham or bacon
2 eggs
4 tbsp self raising flour
2 tbsp oil for frying

Grate the cheese (use a food processor if you have one). Finely chop or grate the onion. Place the cheese and onion in a mixing bowl. Crack the eggs into the bowl, add the flour and ham. Peel and grate the potato then add to the bowl. Mix everything well.

Put the oil in a frying pan (skillet) and set on a medium heat. Using a tablespoon, place dollops of the mixture into the pan. Spread out a little as they will "puff up". You may need to make 2 batches depending on the size of your pan. They will take about 15 minutes to cook but will need turning over every now and then. When the puffs are crispy and golden on all sides they are ready.

This dish is good served with a green vegetable, salad or baked beans in tomato sauce.

PORK CHOPS WITH LIME & COCONUT

Grill (broiler)

Serves 4

Preparation 5 minutes/Cook 20 minutes

Easy to prepare and cook. Tasty too!

4 Pork Chops
2 tbsp creamed coconut
1 lime

Wash the lime, zest it with a sharp knife or zester. Put the zest in a small bowl. Cut the lime in half and squeeze the juice into the bowl. Put the creamed coconut into the bowl. Stir well to combine.

Put the grill (broiler) on. Place the chops on the grill pan and put half the lime and coconut mixture onto the chops. Grill (broil) for about 10 minutes. Turn the chops, add the remaining coconut, lime zest and juice and grill for about 10 more minutes until the skin is crispy and the chops are cooked through.

Serve with mashed potato or potato wedges and green vegetables such as peas, broccoli (calabrese), cabbage or green beans.

SWEET POTATO, SPINACH & CHICKPEAS WITH HALLOUMI

Vegetarian

Hob (stove top)

Serves 4

Preparation 10 minutes/Cook 40 minutes

A one pot meal that is filling and tasty. If you have any leftovers for another day, keep refrigerated until needed then put in a deep ovenproof dish, add some grated cheese and reheat for about 20 minutes until the cheese is bubbling.

8 oz/225g pack of Halloumi cheese
2 lbs/900g/5 cups sweet potatoes
4 oz/100g/4 cups small spinach leaves
16 oz/400g can chickpeas (garbanzo beans)
16 oz/400g can plum tomatoes
3 garlic cloves
1 tbsp tomato purée
1 tbsp oil for frying
Black pepper

Slice the Halloumi cheese into 8 pieces. Peel the sweet potatoes and chop into small chunks. Wash and dry the spinach. Crush the garlic. Put the oil in a casserole or large heavy pan with a lid, add the garlic and stir for a minute or so. Add the sweet potatoes, can of tomatoes, tomato purée, drained chickpeas and pepper. Half fill the empty tomato can with water and add to the pan. Stir and put a lid on. It will take about 30 minutes to cook and will need stirring a few times. Take the lid off during the last 10 minutes of cooking.

When everything is cooked and the sweet potatoes are soft, take the pan off the heat, stir in the spinach, put the lid back on and set aside.

Turn up the heat and put a frying pan (skillet) on to warm through. Add the sliced Halloumi. Fry for 2 minutes on each side until golden. Serve.

SAUSAGE, POTATO & APPLE BAKE

Oven

Serves 4

Preparation 5 minutes/Cook for 45 minutes

Preheat oven to 200C/Fan 180/400F/Gas 6

A winter warmer and quick to prepare.

8 thick sausages
12 oz/350g/2 cups potatoes
1 large onion
6-8 cloves garlic
2 dessert apples
Oil
Salt and black pepper
A handful of herbs e.g. basil, sage or thyme

If using large potatoes, peel and chop into bite sized chunks. If you have new (baby) potatoes, just scrub them in water. Peel and chop the onion into chunks. Leave the garlic cloves unpeeled. Peel, core and slice the apples into quarters.

Drizzle a little oil over the base of a large roasting tin. Add all the ingredients to the tin and mix a few times. Drizzle over a little more oil.

Bake in the oven for about 45 minutes. You will need to take the tin out of the oven a couple of times during cooking to mix and turn everything.

After 45 minutes check that the sausages and potatoes are cooked through and golden. If not, put back in the oven for another 10 minutes.

Serve with green vegetables.

CPSIA information can be obtained at www.ICGtesting.com
Printed in the USA
LVOW02s1436120315

430286LV00003B/55/P